STARS IN MY EYES

EDWARD FIELD

The Sheep Meadow Press
New York City, 1978

ACKNOWLEDGMENTS

"Chopin" appeared in Stand Up, Friend, With Me and is being reprinted by kind permission of Grove Press.

The photographs that appear in this book are courtesy of the Museum of Modern Art Film Stills Archives. My thanks to Valorie Hart for her aid in picture research.

Published by The Sheep Meadow Press
New York, New York

Designed by William Burke
Printed and manufactured in the United States by
the Faculty Press, Inc., Brooklyn, New York
Distributed by Horizon Press, 156 Fifth Avenue, New York, 10010
ISBN # 8180—1537—3
Library of Congress Card Catalog Number 77—95137
First printing

BOOKS BY EDWARD FIELD

Stand Up, Friend, With Me · Grove Press, 1963
Variety Photoplays · Grove Press, 1967
Eskimo Songs and Stories · Delacorte Press, 1973
Sweet Gwendolyn and the Countess · Konglomerati Press, 1976
A Full Heart · Sheep Meadow Press, 1977

CONTENTS

White Jungle Queen

What a girl I was, going in, all innocence,
into the jungle with my father, Dr. Weatherbun.
We were out to explore
the last remaining jungle in All Africa
now that everything else there is like Havana or New York.

But when we arrived
at the edge of the unknown world
of tribes and their gods
the bearers we got from the Real Native Employment Agency
dropped their bales and fled.
"No go there sahib. Bad spirit live there."

I didn't blame them really;
how do people live in such a scary world?
And I thought of my nice lunchcounter job
in Kissin' Trees, Carolina, and Daddy,
that's Dr. Witherspoon, going off every day
to his university job, until the Ford Foundation
gave him this grant; it just shows you
what you can get nowadays if you fill in the application!

Well, without the porters
we had to leave behind all our comforts.
I'd hoped we could sit in armchairs
dressed in cool summer frocks sipping drinks
and watch the natives dancing around the fire.

So we stepped across the magic line
that separates the known from the unknown
where the hungry things live. The very word hungry
sounds like a drooling mouth chomping away at you
and there the gods are always hungry
and the tribes have to keep feeding them like servants.
So when people look at you, they see a roast turkey on a plate.
You are money to them, kind of a currency
they can use to buy something else.

We no sooner stepped into the jungle, the tom-toms started
and we were surrounded, and seized:
Those people paint themselves with eyes all over
so you don't know where to look for the real eyes
and you look at the painted eyes and want to beg them
to spare you, to love you, to stop
thinking what they're thinking! You're good, you really are,
and you would love them if you got the chance
even black as they are,
and me a girl from the South!

So we disappeared into the world beyond sun,
into a nightworld, where laws of sleep run things
and dreams live. I wanted to let go, let go,
and sink into a deeper sleep where the dreaming would stop
but they carried us on to what a girl like me
was never meant to know.
I was ninety-eight pounds of American teen-ager
when I went with my father, Professor Weymouth
on a scientific expedition to explore a jungle.

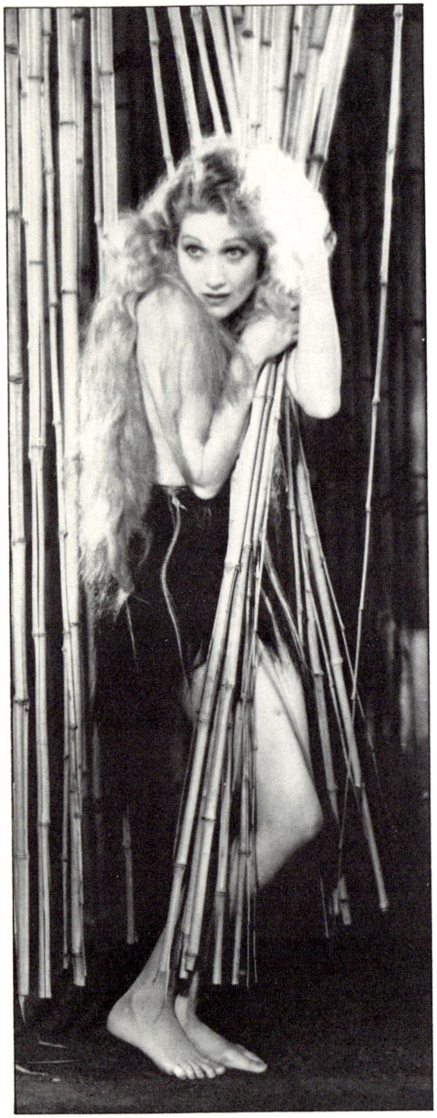

I'll skip the details of how they took us to their village
and put us in a hut: it's exactly like you've seen in the movies.
What happened later was that we got away
by breaking through the wall of the grass hut,
and ran into the jungle;
and the wild beasts came after us like quarry.
They must have got daddy
because I heard somewhere behind me his scream and the growls
and then the grunting of eating and his groans,
and I couldn't listen anymore, I just ran.

I was frantic to get out of the forest:
I could see myself breaking through into the surrounding fields
and heading straight for the port, and staggering home,
and settling down with a good man for life
in Kissin' Trees, Carolina. But it wasn't to be.
I ran until I couldn't run anymore
and my fear led me in circles back to the village.
I think the savages were even watching
and keeping the wild beasts away from me.
They knew what they wanted: a sacrifice for their gods,
or in their language: Karpissu por Kong.

That night they tied me blonde and naked to a stake
piled up with faggots
and started dancing around me to the tom toms:
You can imagine all of them big and shiny with those spears!
It was like the KKK was suddenly all Negroes
and they were in a position to make me pay
for everything awful that had been done them;
and how I would have made up to them for all that if I could,
but not by being burned alive!
Suddenly they seized flaming branches
and threw them on the fuel piled around me
and I prayed and prayed and prayed
as the flames ate their way towards me . . . .
and you know what? There was a crash of thunder
and that show was totally rained out!

Well, the gods had spoken
so they untied me, and laid me swooning on a lion skin,
and made me queen.

The strange thing was I felt the power come over me then,
and their gods were my gods
and I was their white queen in a leopard skin bikini:
Does every southern white girl dream of this?
So of course I stayed: This is my life now.
However, when they do the movie version of my story
I think Elizabeth Taylor should play me, don't you?
I see her in a blonde wig with hair tumbling to her knees.
I'm writing the screenplay myself.

Can't you just see me at the world premiere in Hollywood
in my leopard skin nothings and marching behind me
my tall tribe of warriors, every one of them a beauty?
That's my only dream.
Anyway, until then I'm not in any pain,
if you get what I mean honey.
(Akimba darling, get me another mango.)
All I have to do is lie back and wait for Hollywood to call.

Frankenstein

The monster has escaped from the dungeon
where he was kept by the Baron
who made him with knobs sticking out from each side of his neck
where the head was attached to the body
and stitching all over
where parts of cadavers were sewed together.

He is pursued by the ignorant villagers
who think he is evil and dangerous because he is ugly
and makes ugly noises.
They wave fire-brands at him and cudgels and rakes,
but he escapes and comes to the thatched cottage
of an old blind man playing on the violin Mendelssohn's Spring Song.

Hearing him approach, the blind man welcomes him:
"Come in, my friend," and takes him by the arm.
"You must be weary," and sits him down inside the house.
For the blind man has long dreamed of having a friend
to share his lonely life.

The monster has never known kindness — the Baron was cruel —
but somehow he is able to accept it now,
and he really has no instincts to harm the old man,
for in spite of his awful looks he has a tender heart:
Who knows what cadaver that part of him came from.

The old man seats him at table, offers him bread,
and says, "Eat, my friend." The monster
rears back roaring in terror.
"No, my friend, it is good. Eat — good,"
and the old man shows him how to eat,
and reassured, the monster eats
and says, "Eat — good,"
trying out the words and finding them good too.

The old man offers him a glass of wine,
"Drink, my friend. Drink — good."
The monster drinks, slurping horribly, and says
"Drink — good" in his deep nutty voice
and smiles maybe for the first time in his life.

Then the blind man puts a cigar in the monster's mouth
and lights a large wooden match that flares up in his face.
The monster, remembering the torches of the villagers,
recoils, grunting in terror.
"No, my friend, smoke — good,"
and the old man demonstrates with his own cigar.
The monster takes a tentative puff
and smiles hugely, saying, "Smoke — good,"
and sits back like a banker, grunting and puffing.

Now the old man plays Mendelssohn's Spring Song on the violin
while tears came into our dear monster's eyes
as he thinks of the stones of the mob, the pleasures of mealtime,
the magic new words he has learned
and above all of the friend he has found.

It is just as well that he is unaware,
being simple enough to believe only in the present,
that the mob will find him and pursue him
for the rest of his short unnatural life
until trapped at the whirlpool's edge
he plunges to his death.

Whatever Happened to May Caspar?

What happens to old movie stars,
those faded queens of stage and screen?
They move into hotels off Times Square maybe
where they live among their souvenirs,
near the lights, the people, the premieres
that no longer know them —
funny old ladies with hair a pink frizz,
salvaging old costumes for street clothes.

Does anyone remember May Caspar now?
She was all the rage in thirty-three
when she starred in "May Morning" with Ronald Peale,
in which she played a simple country girl
and he a prince who lost his heart among the apple blossoms.

Now thirty years later (that makes her about sixty, at least),
what does she see when she sits down to her vanity table
with its clutter of lotions?
Does she stare at the blur in the mirror
and remember how young she was in that movie,
how pure and fragile?
Before she puts on her glasses
she takes a swig out of a large perfume bottle,
and goes about painting a kewpie doll over the wreck of her face:
Somehow it always comes out crooked.

Later, after her disastrous marriage to Nick Kinsella
and the divorce and the operations
(they say he beat her up horribly),
after she got back her looks,
she played femme fatale roles on divans with heavy eye make-up.
Remember "A Woman's Eyes," with Ivan Carlovan,
in which May was the toast of Vienna
until the love of her prince turned to hate
when he discovered a stableboy was her lover
and she had to flee through snowdrifts in a sleigh
standing up behind the horses singing:
                    The heart will find a way

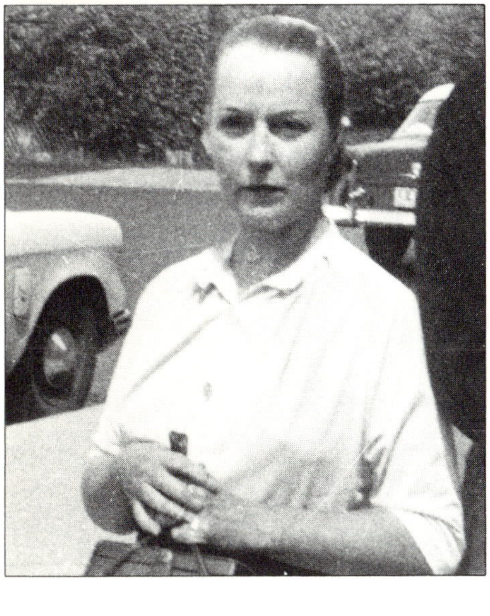

but ending up in a waterfront bar in Marseilles
singing with an accordion:
A woman's eyes are pools of sin.
Don't look too long, they'll lure you in.
There were dozens of suicides to her record of that song.

Then came her greatest hit "The Downward Path"
in which she played a mature stage star
who fell in love with a young actor,
but he only used her to make it to the top
while she went downhill fast and ended in the gutter
selling flowers by the stage door
as he came out with the ingenue on his arm,
and stepped into the waiting limousine.

How her beautiful eyes shone in that scene!
You knew she held no grudge, but loved him still
as she sang after him:

Go, beautiful youth,
forget me now, for I am old.
Enjoy your fame as I did mine.
For that, America forgave her everything,
her parade of unsuitable husbands,
her drunken brawls in restaurants.
She was darling May Caspar, for a few years anyway,
(her career lasted only three years),
then she faded away.

Now forgotten, she is that funny old lady
living shabbily on a dwindling income
in a Times Square hotel, once genteel,
now full of call girls and Kansas tourists.
It gets harder and harder to pay the bills.
Back rent mounts up. Room service is cut off.
She lives on hot dogs. Her fate looks grim.

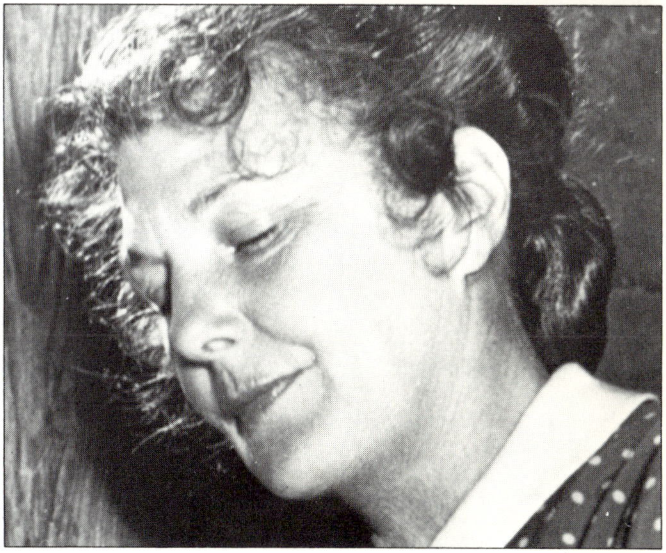

She is about to be put out in the street
with her souvenirs and wardrobe
for the winter wind to blow away,
plumes and bits of fur and photographs and dried corsages,
and she skittering after them down the streets.

But wait, here comes a late rider:
A message from the Museum of Modern Art!
They are planning a May Caspar revival
and she is wanted to appear in person, like the old days.
May Caspar movies stamped Authentic American Art.
She is proclaimed A Great Actress.
May Caspar Called Back to Hollywood to Make Film.
But first she goes to Last Chance,
exclusive beauty resort in Death Valley
where they go to work on her
with hormones, vitamins, embryo implants, and surgery.

When she shows up in Hollywood her beauty is restored.
Thirty years of ravagement have been erased:
There is not a wrinkle.
Of course her strength is not what it was —
two men have to hold her up,
but she is a great trouper and the show will go on.
Today they are filming her big scene on the divan, her trademark:
Lights, Camera, Action: May Caspar acts again!

Anyway she tries, but the effort is too much for her:
the hot lights, the excitement,
her skin held taut by invisible clips,
her heart stimulated with drugs,
her head sweating under the wig,
every bit of her is held together with string and sealing wax.

"Okay Miss Caspar, give it all you've got."
The camera moves in inexorably for the closeup.
She tries desperately to think young, to hold everything up.
Those merciless lights!
Too late, it all collapses.

Goodbye May Caspar.
We loved you
in the way we love —
faithlessly.
Or are we, growing older,
ready to remember again
our great loves
of yesteryear
and go search for them
where we lost sight of them
in those shabby places,
close to the brightest
lights
that cast the deepest
shadow?

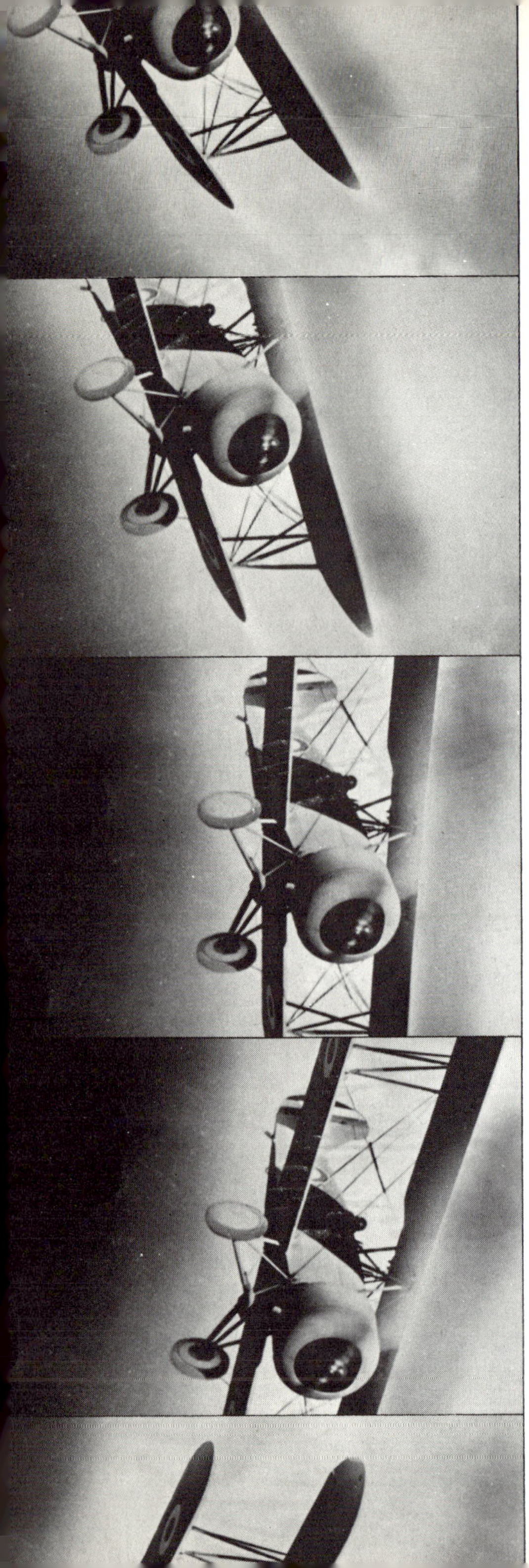

The Tailspin

Going into a tailspin
in those days meant curtains.
No matter how hard you pulled back on the stick
the nose of the plane wouldn't come up.

Spinning round, headed for a target of earth,
the whine of death in the wing-struts,
instinct made you try to pull out of it that way, by force,
and for years aviators spiraled down and crashed.

Who could have dreamed that the solution
to this dreaded aeronautical problem
was so simple?
Every student flyer learns this nowadays:
you move the joystick in the direction of the spin
and like a miracle the plane stops turning
and you are in control again
to pull the nose up out of the dive.

In panic we want to push the stick away from the spin,
wrestle the plane out of it,
but the trick is, as in everything,
to go with the turning willingly,
rather than fight, give in, go with it,
and that way come out of your tailspin whole.

Chopin

Chopin is such a great composer
I can even write poetry while his music is on the radio
which is unusual for me.
He makes my fingers nimble like ballerinas on the keys.
He says, Let's go to town slambang on the whole goddam machine.

I love you Chopin in spite of the million fingers
of little girls with long bobbing curls
practicing your notes during daylight hours
but mostly three to five after school.
You set the hands of the children of the world
grubbing at the keyboard
like Pavlova put them on their wobbly toes.

I love you Chopin in spite of Merle Oberon
although that was a pretty good movie where sweet Paul Muni
still had two good eyes to see you were a genius.
I liked how he made you fight for Polish nationalism
that dead duck with two heads;
but of course really he was urging you
not to turn over the Jews to the Germans
and your fingers flew like mad to save them,
but you couldn't save them since piano playing
never saves anyone except the player if he's cute besides
(like Van Cliburn walking through the iron curtain).
Anyway when my mother was a girl in Poland
it had become a nation already, a nation of Jewhaters
so it couldn't have been the result of your gorgeous music
which clearly says, Love the Jews.

Chopin, my soul,
don't listen to those critics with their dried-up eyes;
they don't like me either, my poems embarrass them.
You are too good for them
so if they want to snub you, let them,
let them miss out on all the fun in life
like making love and dancing about and being Mediterranean,
still acting silly and uncynical like sixteen,
like promising to love forever and ever and doing it.

A Film Scenario:

Lower East Side

The George Bernstein Story

It starts on the Lower East Side
when Irving Berlin, Fanny Brice, Paul Muni,
all the bigshots in show business, the underworld,
politics, and the arts,
were still rollerskating among the pushcarts,
and calling up Hey Ma for a penny to be thrown down
and if no penny fell, going off to earn one by their talents.

Just off the boat the Bernsteins arrive
corner Delancey and Orchard, greenhorns,
Mama with her big pot,
Papa looking for a sweatshop to work in,
and the kids Sammy and Ethel saying Gee Whiz
and eating their first bananas that tasted funny to them.

They settle in a cold-water flat
(nine dollars a month in those days —
now ninety if you qualify professional)
in a tenement that is multi-racial rather than inter-racial
(meaning no Colored):
an Irish woman on the top floor
with two sons, one a gangster and the other a cop,
her sorrow being that she didn't have a third to be a priest
and that way cover all possible professions;
and a German couple running the candy store downstairs,
who later go back to Germany with photographs of the neighborhood
and a complete list of the Jews there for the master file.

Life goes on, the good times and the bad:
Papa right away organizes the workers
and they go out on strike.
Little Sammy reads Tolstoy and Marx
and becomes a hothead radical and argues.
He goes around singing:

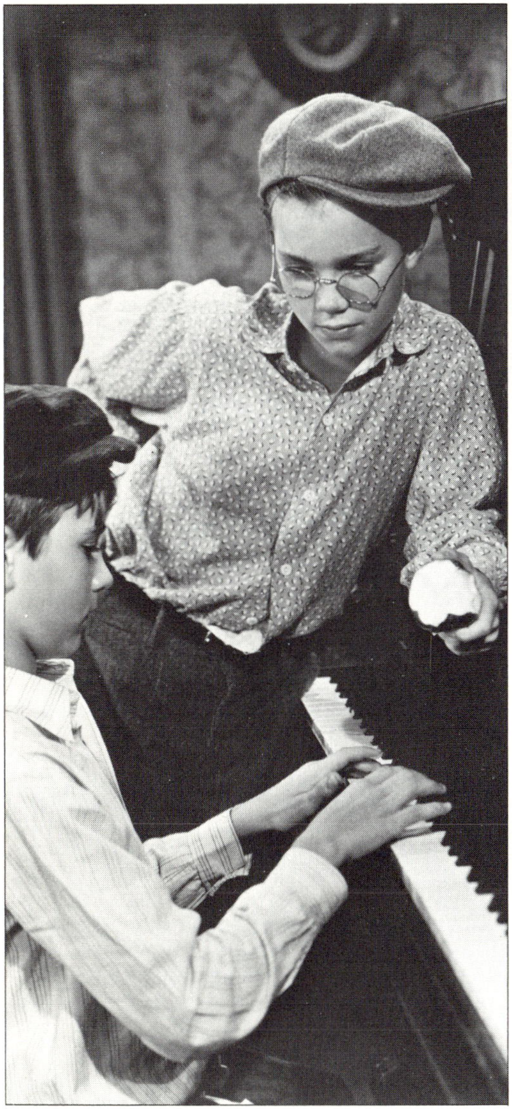

The hat workers union
is a fascist union,
the hat workers union
is a fascist union,
they preach socialism
but they practice fascism
to make the world better for the boss class.

At last George our hero is born, the fruit of freedom
and settles down to his music lessons,
with the family standing around beaming
as he plays Minuet in G.

Before long he is sneaking out of the house nights.
For crime? No. After girls? No,
he was playing piano for the silent films.
(What am I saying films, nowadays they're films,
then they were movies.)

His father is furious when he learns about this:
George was only supposed to play religious music.
Sammy and Ethel were the secular wing of the family.
What was all this about jazz? That is music?
But playing organ in the synagogue one Friday night
George fell to dreaming and broke into ragtime,
and pretty soon all those old bearded Jews
are tapping their feet and smiling.
So George is kicked out into the hard world
with no blessing from his father except "You bum you"
and makes the rounds of Tin Pan Alley.

Sammy the oldest gives up Karl Marx
and marries a merchant's ugly daughter
and gets rich working in the business
and moves away to a better-class neighborhood like Brooklyn.

Little Ethel is growing up smart too,
and the struggling student who loves her
can hardly offer her the good times she had a right to
with her face and figure.
Pretty soon she is being driven home in a long limousine with curtains.
It pulled right up to the tenement door
with the neighbors staring from stoops and windows.
She drew a heavy veil over her face
and went up to the kitchen
where Ma turns a stone face to the stove.

"Look at you Ma," she says, "you're only forty.
I don't want that to happen to me,
so I'm getting out of this dump."
And she goes off to be kept by the Irish woman's gangster son
who was making a million as a bootlegger.

George writes song hit after song hit
and meets Alexis Smith, a noble society woman with ice-blond hair
who comes to his mother's house Friday nights
for the chicken soup and matzoh balls.
"You know Mother Bernstein, uptown we don't get food like this."
Anyway her French chef doesn't make it.
After about ten years engagement
she gives George up because
she doesn't want to stand in the way of his music.

Meanwhile Ethel has been secretly putting her student through school
and paying the doctor bills for his crippled sister
who wants to be a ballet dancer if the operation turns out successful.
But her gangster finally gets killed by his cop brother
when he comes, a fugitive, to his mother's kitchen door
and begs her to hide him from the law, and she says no.
He is then shot dead on the fire-escape in the searchlights,
his blood dripping down on the elegant clothes of Ethel weeping below.

So Ethel comes back home and marries her student, now a lawyer,
but their first child is born dead
and the doctor says she will never be able to have another,
because of her past sins.

More success for George, in London and Paris,
command performance, cheering crowds, grey hair:
Tonight his great musical LOWER EAST SIDE is opening
and it looks like a hit.
His leading lady loves him
but he always says, "As long as mama is alive . . ."

The curtain is about to go up on Act Three.
A telegram comes, his manager reads it:
PAPA HIT BY CAR, MOMMA HAS HEART ATTACK, COME AT ONCE. ETHEL.
The manager asks himself, Should I show it to him now?
George is standing in the wings ready to go out
and sing the finale himself.
His manager gives him the telegram.
He reads it as the orchestra plays the introduction, his cue.
The orchestra plays it again, and the audience starts murmuring.
George staggers out on stage humbly,
a small man with tears in his eyes,
holding the fatal telegram in his hand;
and looking up at the brightest light
that makes the tears click down his cheeks like diamonds,
he sings his big song.

Thunderous applause, cheers, rave reviews:
He takes the train to the funeral.
Standing around the grave, Ethel, Sammy, himself,
all grown up now, well-dressed.
The old kitchen, oilcloth table top,
mama's pot she could always make soup in just by adding water.
What happened? Where did we go wrong?
Ethel and Sammy go away in their limousines:
"Got to be running along, kid. Call me sometime."
Alone. Mama, Papa, where are you?
Tears. A hand falls on his shoulder. His manager.
He looks long into the loving eyes. He decides.

He puts a coin in the pay phone: "Darling,
I want you to marry me, I love you."
He is calling his leading lady who has long loved him.
"Oh George" she breathes, as the music
whirls up into a symphony of hearts full of happiness
and the lovers rush into each other's arms in the middle of the stage
to sing the grand finale:
LOWER EAST SIDE.

The Bride of Frankenstein

The baron has decided to mate the monster,
to breed him perhaps,
in the interests of pure science, his only god.

So he goes up into his laboratory
which he has built in the tower of the castle
to be as near the interplanetary forces as possible,
and puts together the prettiest monster-woman you ever saw
with a body like a pin-up girl
and hardly any stitching at all
where he sewed on the head of a raped and murdered beauty queen.

He sets his liquids burping, and coils blinking and buzzing,
and waits for an electric storm to send through the equipment
the spark vital for life.
The storm breaks over the castle
and the equipment really goes crazy
like a kitchen full of modern appliances
as the lightning juice starts oozing right into that pretty corpse.

He goes to get the monster
so he will be right there when she opens his eyes,
for she might fall in love with the first thing she sees
as ducklings do.
That monster is already straining at his chains and slurping
ready to go right to it:
He has been well prepared for coupling
by his pinching leering keeper who's been saying for weeks,
"You gonna get a little nookie, kid,"
or "How do you go for some poontag, baby."
All the evil in him is focused on this one thing now
as he is led into her very presence.

She awakens slowly,
she bats her eyes,
she gets up out of the equipment,
and finally she stands in all her seamed glory,
a monster princess with a hairdo like a fright-wig,
lightning flashing in the background
like a halo and a wedding veil,
like a photographer snapping pictures of great moments.

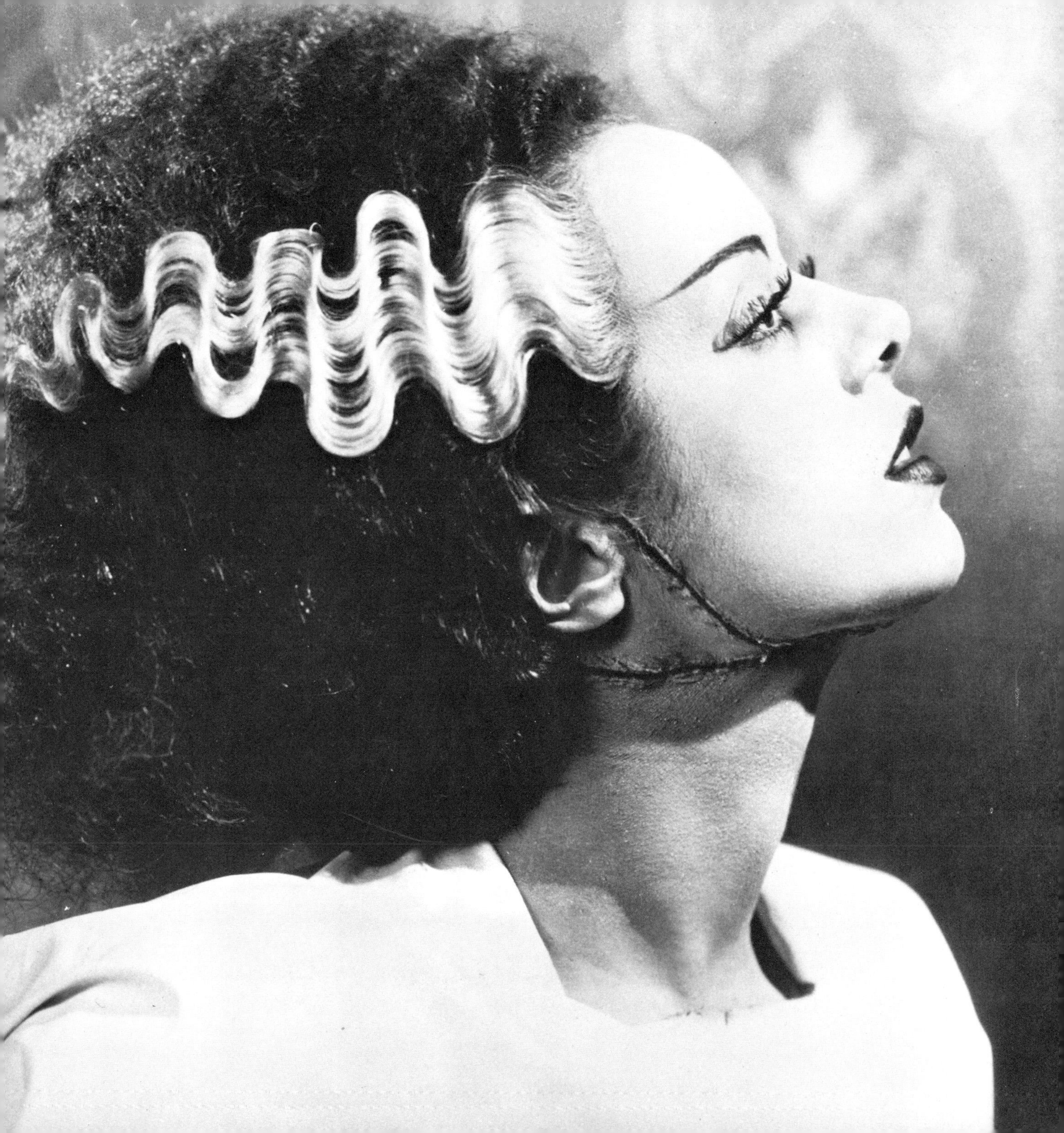

She stands and stares with her electric eyes,
beginning to understand that in this life too
she was just another body to be raped.

The monster is ready to go:
He roars with joy at the sight of her,
so they let him loose and he goes right for those knockers.
And she starts screaming to break your heart
and you realize that she was just born:
In spite of her big tits she was just a baby.

But her instincts are right —
rather death than that green slobber:
She jumps off the parapet.
And then the monster's sex drive goes wild.
Thwarted, it turns to violence, demonstrating sublimation crudely,
and he wrecks the lab, those burping acids and buzzing coils,
overturning the control panel so the equipment goes off like a bomb,
the stone castle crumbling and crashing in the storm
destroying them all . . . . perhaps.

Perhaps somehow the baron got out of that wreckage of his dreams
with his evil intact if not his good looks
and more wicked than ever went on with his thrilling career.

And perhaps even the monster lived
to roam the earth, his desire still ungratified,
and lovers out walking in shadowy and deserted places
will see his shape loom up over them, their doom —
and children sleeping in their beds
will wake up in the dark night screaming
as his hideous body grabs them.

The Curse of the Cat Woman

It sometimes happens
that the woman you meet and fall in love with
is of that strange Transylvanian people
with an affinity for cats.

You take her to a restaurant, say, or a show,
on an ordinary date, being attracted
by the glitter in her slitty eyes and her cat-like walk,
and afterwards of course you take her in your arms
and she turns into a black panther
and bites you to death.

Or perhaps you are saved in the nick of time
and she is tormented by the knowledge of her tendency:
That she daren't hug a man
unless she wants to risk clawing him up.

This puts you both in a difficult position,
panting lovers who are prevented from touching,
not by bars but by circumstance:
You have terrible fights and say cruel things
for having the hots does not give you a sweet temper.

One night you are walking down a dark street
and hear the pad-pad of a panther following you,
but turning around there are only shadows,
or perhaps one shadow too many.

You approach, calling "Who's there?"
and it leaps on you.
Luckily you have brought along your sword
and you stab it to death.

And before your eyes it turns into the woman you love,
her breast impaled on your sword,
her mouth dribbling blood saying she loved you
but couldn't help her tendency.

So death released her from the curse at last
and you knew from the angelic smile on her dead face
that in spite of a life the devil owned,
love had won, and heaven pardoned her.

The Life of Joan Crawford

for Barbara Barry

She was a working girl from a small town
but the town wasn't so small
that it didn't have a railroad track
dividing the right side from the wrong side.
On the right side was the Hill
where the swells lived in big houses,
and on the wrong side, the Hollow where the proletariat
spent their greasy and unrewarding lives.
(For in those days the American town
was a living demonstration of Marxist theory.)

Joan of course lived in the hollow
in one of those shacks with sagging porches
the mill put up rows of for the workers.
Her father, Tim Crawford, was the town drunk
living on relief and odd jobs
ever since the mines closed down when Joan was a baby.
He had been waiting for them to reopen for twenty years.
Joan never knew what had happened to her mother.
Joan's birth, her mother's disappearance or death, the mine's closing,
that was in a time of violence no one would discuss.
Just mention it and her father went on a binge,
not that he was ever sober.

She sighed, and went off to work in the five and ten
wearing her made-over dress with little washable collar and cuffs.
Even with her prole accent and the cheap bag and shoes
she was a good looker.
Men used to come by in their flashy suits and big cigars,
call her tootsie and ask her for a date,
but she knew a poor girl didn't stand a chance with them.
She wasn't one of those innocents
who think a guy loves you if he gets a hard-on.
Yet she wouldn't go with any of the boys from the hollow either
because with them the future was sleazy with kids
and the ruin of her figure before she was thirty —
and no fun after the honeymoon
except the Friday-night fight
when he would come home stinking, having drunk up the paycheck
and beat her black and blue
when she threw the stack of overdue bills at him —
and then screw her viciously on the dining-room table.
Some fun.
That was life in the hollow and she wasn't having any.
She had turned down a job working in the mill
where the pay was better but life closed like a trap on you
and chose the more lady-like job at the five and ten
where people called her Miss and she could pose genteely
behind the Tangee cosmetic display and the ribbon counter.
For Joan had the makings of a lady
if she could ever get some dough to fix herself up with
and a speech teacher to correct her dreadful accent.

But Nature had its way with Joan at last:
Spring came and handsome John Wainrich
(of the best family in town — they owned everything,
the five and dime, the shut mines, and the mill) —
John Wainrich came in one day to collect the receipts or something
and found a million dollar baby in his own five and ten cents store.
Well Joan fell hard
and went out with him in his big car
and of course in the moonlight she let him have his way with her.

She used to meet him on the sly
when he could get away from the country club
and the milk-white debutante he was engaged to,
and they would drive out to road-houses
where he wouldn't be seen by his swell friends.
Joan had pride,
but what is a woman's pride when she's in love.
What it came to, a few months later,
was that she got pregnant,
and just as she was about the break the good news,
he told her he was going to be married
and would have to stop seeing her until after the wedding,
that it was just a marriage of convenience
and wouldn't make any difference to them.
So she couldn't tell him then, she would have died first.

My great love, she muttered sarcastically,
He didn't even use a scum-bag.
And she went off to the city
where she got a job as receptionist in an office.
Her boss, Mr. Harris, was an older but dignified man
with a wife at home on Park Avenue, the victim of neurosis and wealth:
with all that money she could buy neither health nor happiness.
Joan used to listen to Mr. Harris's troubles
when she brought him his alka-seltzer mornings.
And when she was promoted to secretary, they would have dinner out
and she'd advise him on business,
she being a girl with a good head on her shoulders.

In Mr. Harris's company she saw the world and learned fast.
She lost her small-town look and learned to dress,
wearing hat and gloves, to fluff out her hair
and drink vermouth cocktails and ride in cabs.
And while retaining the colorful idiom of the Hollow,
her grammar improved, and her voice lost its nasal whine.
Joan was a knockout in every way
from honest eyes and square shoulders
to the narrow hips of a tango dancer.

Nothing showed yet in the baby department.
At night Joan looked critically at herself in the mirror:
Not a bulge, but baby was in there all right,
and her eyes went bitter as she thought of its father —
her great love, hmph.
"Well young feller, at least we'll have each other.
But I'd better be making preparations.
A working girl can't leave things to the caterer."

Then her boss proposed: he'd divorce his wife and marry her.
"Gee Mr. Harris, I think you're swell but I can't.
There is a real big favor you could do for me, though,"
and she told him all, how she gave her all for love
and her lover turned out to be a louse.
So Mr. Harris set her up in a little flat until the baby came.
He didn't make any demands on her or anything,
not yet anyway: it was sort of a promissory note
to be paid off later when she grew to love him out of gratitude.

But her ex-lover, John Wainrich, came to town
with his new wedding ring on, and tracked her down;
and misunderstanding the arrangement, called her a few names,
but swore she was his and he'd never give her up.
Joan still loved him but had the courage
to flee to a cheap hotel.
She got a job as a dance-hall hostess, dime-a-dance,
six months pregnant, but with a brave smile
as the customers stepped on her toes.
They found her a good joe and a willing ear
as they told her their troubles
while rubbing off against her to a slow foxtrot.
One of her customers, impressed by her dancing,
got her to enter a dance marathon with him for prize money —
she needed that dough for the little stranger —
but the strain was too much for her,
marathon-dancing in her seventh month!

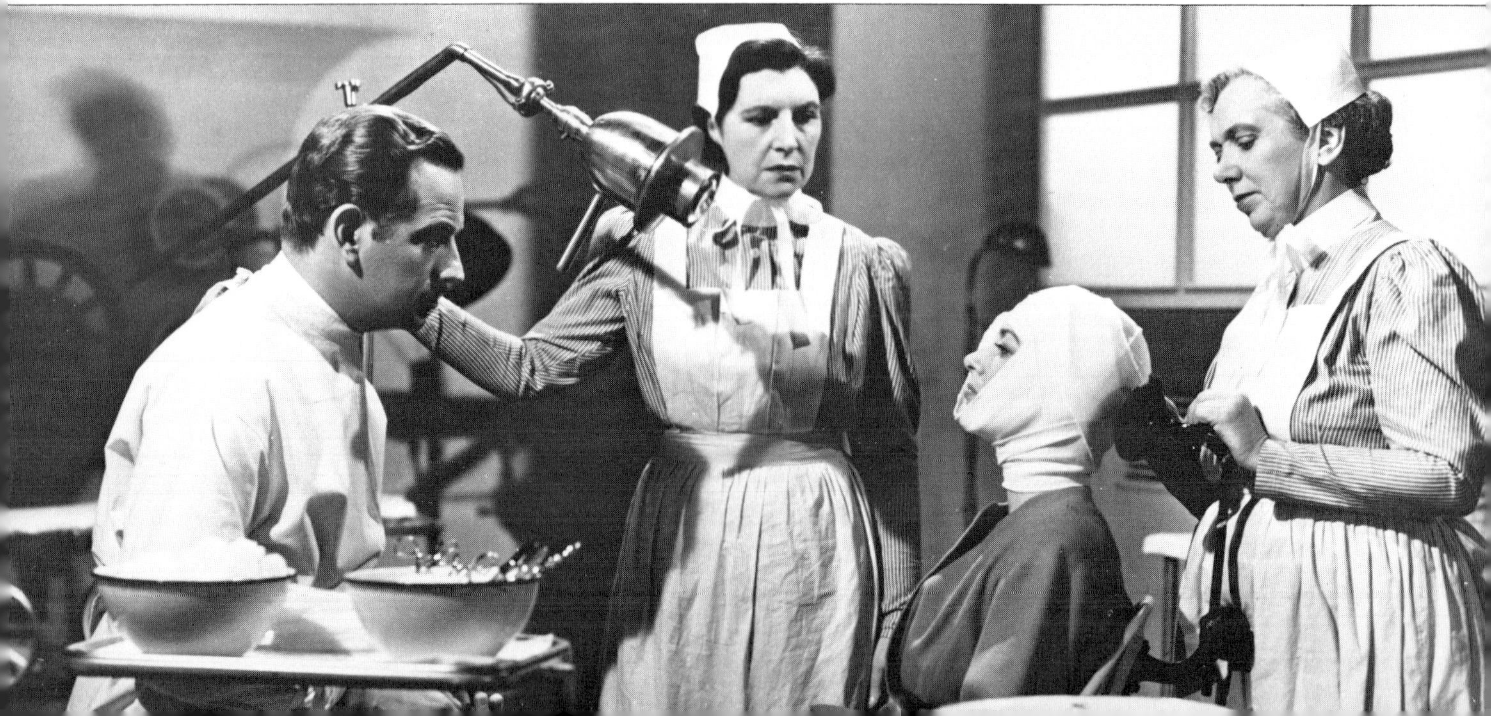

She came to on a hospital bed
with no makeup on and a white cloth over her forehead like a nun
to see her griddle-faced father looking down on her,
his mouth boozy as ever, but in his heart
vowing to go on the wagon if God would spare her life:
"Come home with me, Joanie, I'll take care of you."
"And baby too, papa?"
"Didn't they tell you, Joanie? The baby . . ."
"Oh no . . ."
And tears of mourning still in her eyes
she went back home to the Hollow and kept house for her father.

She had two visits shortly after returning home:
First, John's pale bride came by, big with child,
neglect driving her to seek out her rival.
When she saw Joan so sweet and good
instead of some tramp homewrecker type,
she burst into tears and confessed she knew John didn't love her
but hoped he would when the baby was born, his heir.
The bitterness in Joan's heart turned to pity —
Weren't they both women who had suffered? —
so she forgave her and they wept together:
Joan never could resist being a pal.

The other visit was from old Mr. Wainrich, John's father.
(Never had the Hollow seen so many long cars drive through.)
The old capitalist had a confession to make:
"When I saw you at the window watering the geraniums
I could have sworn you were your mother."

"You knew my mother, Mr. Wainrich?" asked Joan astonished.
"Yes. Bette wasn't like the other women in the Hollow.
She was a Davis you know. Her parents
had been plantation people down in Georgia
and even if they did end up here in the Hollow
she never forgot that she was a thoroughbred."
"Are you trying to tell me that you loved my mother?" Joan gasped.

"Yes, I loved her, but the heir to an industrial empire
isn't free to marry whom he chooses,
so my family chose an appropriate bride for me.
At that time I was running our coal-mines here,
where Tim Crawford worked.
He was the biggest and toughest man in the Hollow
so naturally he was spokesman for the boys.
He had loved your mother for years
but she knew what it meant for a woman to marry a miner
and live in constant fear of a cave-in.
And she hated his coarse language and crude manners: she was a lady.
And besides, she loved me.
But when I broke the news of my engagement to her
(I explained it was just a marriage of convenience
and it wouldn't make any difference to us)
she married Tim just to spite me.
But it wasn't enough for her: right on my wedding day
she got Tim Crawford to call the men out on strike
and with violence surging around the Hill,
I had the biggest wedding ever seen in these parts.
I was coal and my bride was steel: what a merger!
The President came, and there were reporters from Chicago,
and your mother, already big with child, leading a picket line.

That strike went on for months, and you were born in the middle of it.
But we couldn't go on apart, your mother and I.
We knew we were sinners, but we managed to meet on the sly,
although the strike had turned the town into a battlefield
and we belonged to opposing armies.
Finally we decided to run away together, but just at that time
a load of scabs I was importing to work the mines arrived,
and there was a tremendous battle between them and the miners,
led by Tim Crawford of course.
The miners had lead pipes and dynamite,
but we had the National Guard in full battle dress.
Your mother and I, eloping, got caught in the middle
and took refuge in a deserted mine;
and I don't know which side did it, but a stick of dynamite
was thrown down the shaft, and your mother
was buried by a ton of falling rock."

Joan moaned and hid her face in her hands.
"It was useless to do anything so I left her there.
Why say anything when no one knew?
She was destroyed by the strike she had started.
The mines were shut down for good of course,
I couldn't bear the memory.
They would have had to be shut anyway,
we were losing money on them."
"And that's why daddy never knew what happened to mother,
raising me all by himself, and took to drink . . ."
"Yes, and I went back to my wife and our little John was born
and I tried to forget . . ."
"Promise me one thing, Mr. Wainrich," Joan said,
"for the sake of my mother's memory,
that you'll open the mines again and give daddy back his old job."

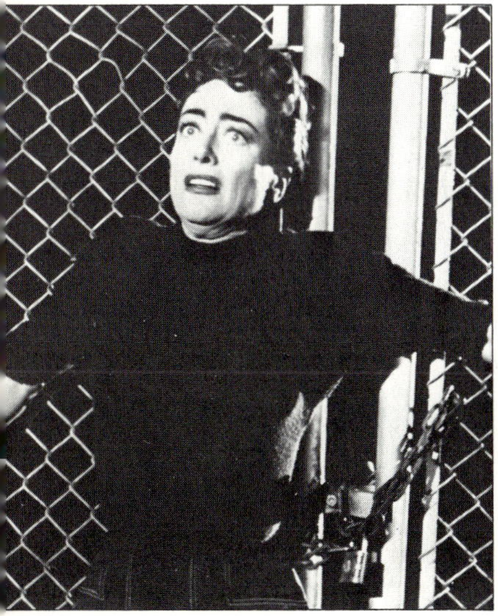

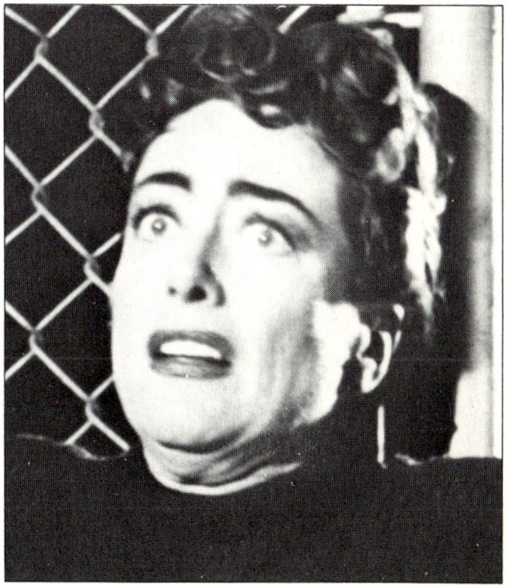

Joan had a lot to think about in the days that followed.
One day she got a call to come up right away to the big house,
and arriving, found John's wife dying,
having given birth to a child, and asking for her.
The pale bride lay holding her child, the Wainrich heir,
but seeing Joan, she sat up with her last strength and said,
"I give him to you," and fell back dead.
Joan fainted away, and when she came to,
it seemed a long time later, after the funeral and the mourning,
John Wainrich held her in his arms and was saying over and over,
"I am yours now, she gave me to you."
"But she meant the child," Joan cried.
"Both of us are yours, my darling."

So Joan found her place in life at last.
They always said she'd make it up there, surrounded by the help,
a lady, moving gracefully among the guests.
And what a difference now:
the miners in tuxes standing around the punchbowl with the swells,
the colored butler joining in the fun with loud yaks,
a new era, the classless society,
brought about the smartest little woman in the USA,

Ladies and Gentlemen: Miss Joan Crawford.

Mae West

She comes on drenched in a perfume called Self-Satisfaction
from feather boa to silver pumps.

She does not need to be loved by you
though she'll give you credit for good taste.
Just because you say you love her
she's not throwing herself at your feet in gratitude.

Every other star reveals how worthless she feels
by crying when the hero says he loves her,
or how unhoped-for the approval is
when the audience applauds her big number —
but Mae West takes it as her due:
She knows she's good.

She expects the best for herself
and knows she's worth what she costs
and she costs plenty —
she's not giving anything away.

She enjoys her admirers, fat daddy or muscleman,
and doesn't confuse vanity and sex,
though she never turns down pleasure,
lapping it up.

Above all she enjoys her self,
swinging her body that says, Me, me, me, me,
Why not have a good time?
As long as you amuse me, go on,
I like you slobbering over my hand, big boy —
I have a right to.

Most convincing, we know all this
not by her preaching it
but by her presence — it's no act.
Every word and look and movement
spells independence:
She likes being herself.

And we who don't
can only look on, astonished.

Sonja Henie Sonnet

In high school we danced the lindy white-style
like Sonja Henie on her skates
curvetting her way around the rinky-dink
back-first, front-first, leaving a trail of scars.

Splitting in air or dissolving in a spin
she came out holding her muff to cheeks
dimpled and rosy under bo-peep bonnet
as snowflakes starred her blond and marcelled head,

and curtsying, her little behind
peek-a-booed under fluffy skirt
when she braked to a stop before the cameras
in a cloud of powdery ice.

Below, blunt feet in leather with blades of steel
dug in their points and held.

She

You are on an expedition for a museum
following rumors of a lost civilization
in the far north among the ice mountains.

You come across a block of ice
with a sabre-tooth tiger frozen in it like a sentinel
and you know you are near.
For with a supply of fresh-frozen meat like that
man can survive in these parts.
Then you find frozen in the ice
some earlier explorers who disappeared.
The expression on their faces says
nothing pleasant is ahead.

A convenient avalanche opens a passageway
that leads into the lost kingdom.
You are seized and brought before the queen,
SHE, a young and beautiful girl.

You see her and love her
and SHE wants you to rule forever at her side,
so SHE shows you her secret,
a magic fire that keeps her young,
for SHE is really a thousand years old, SHE confesses.
SHE has to step into the fire once a year:
It's time right now in fact.

You realize you have been taken in by an old lady,
you, who are only capable of loving youth —
and anyway SHE's no virgin, having had as many lovers as years
and killing them finally when SHE was tired of them.
Really, was it the new lovers or the fire that kept her young?

SHE said, "Wait a minute while I take my annual fire bath."
You are horrified — SHE is a monster and a tyrant —
and you stamp out the fire
and before your eyes time catches up with her,
and SHE ages into a hag, that beauty you just kissed,
crumples, dies, rots, dries up, and turns to dust,
a thousand years passing before your eyes.

No time to lose, for time was catching up with the kingdom too:
You make your escape to the present
just as the corridors of ice crash down behind you
obliterating once and for all all trace of SHE and her world,
and you stand safely outside on the edge of that avalanche.

Back in London at the museum
you stand around with colleagues in evening clothes
in front of a glass case holding a stuffed sabre-tooth tiger.
"Magnificent specimen, that," Lord Avon says.
"Let me tell you the story," you say.
"Perhaps you will find it unbelievable but every word is true,"
as a mist of memory, of youth forever lost
comes over your blue eyes.

Book of the Dead

An island in the fog. Waves lapping.
Strange movements. Figures digging graves.
Our boat approaches silently.
We have come to rescue the girl Divina
from the mad doctor
who uses the blood of virgins
for a serum to restore his wife's beauty,
poor Madame Imperia who always wears a mask
imploring him to work harder, cursing her fate.

He has an army of half-human slaves,
their brains replaced by those of dogs,
and a chief assistant Igor,
whose mother was a Siberian witch
and his father a British scientist on an expedition
to locate frozen mammoths
for a meat-packing concern.
Igor rules the army of dogmen
with a whip and a sharp boot in the butt.

Now as we come nearer there is the sound
of barking voices, shovels on stone,
and an occasional yelping
as Igor kicks a lazy cur in the ribs
or the whip separates snarling mad dogmen
going for each others' throats.

Are we too late?
Have they already drained Divina's blood
for the vain Madame Imperia
to make her young again?
The boat slips into the cove,
we gather up the equipment for the rescue
and steal into the woods around the house
of mad doctor Cranshaw,
a benevolent-looking dwarf from Groton, Massachusetts,

who fell into the clutches of Madame Imperia.
She had chosen him
because of his high marks in chemistry at M.I.T.
and his personal fortune
for she knew that getting back your looks costs plenty.
They were married at a society wedding in Newport
after which she took off her undetectable plastic face
and showed him her true one, so horrible
that he bought the island and set up a laboratory there
to search for a lotion
that would restore her beauty.

Now for twenty years girls had been disappearing
until most recently our heroine Divina
was snatched from her prayers
at the grotto of Our Lady of Loreto.

At first everyone supposed she had run off to be a hippy.
That's where girls used to go,
into the international druggy scene
until they turned up in a basement dead
from the O.D.'s with tracks up and down their arms,
or sometimes with two little teeth marks at the throat
and strangely drained of blood.
Divina had dropped acid a few times
but she was no junkie,
and she was into the I Ching and the Jesus prayer
but she was no hippy.
Anyway, nobody is a hippy anymore.
Nowadays girls go into the feminist movement,
and if they disappear, it's into the radical lesbian underground
holding up banks and blowing up bridges.

Well, Divina had swung a little both ways—
we both led a hip life-style—
but she was no dyke, I'll swear to that.
She was really crazy about me, if you know what I mean—
she was my chick, she was in trouble,
so the Chief assigned me to the case:
It was ready Eddie to the rescue!

Now we were approaching the house through the dark trees,
brushing away cobwebs from our faces, ugh.
In a clearing ahead two dogmen carried something
horrible and writhing off into the bushes.
Inside the house through the lighted window
the doctor was experimenting on one of the dogmen.
Everybody was busy at his tasks
except Madame Imperia
who only sat around veiled and cursing,
ordering the dogmen to bring her this and that,
polishing her nails, and filing them razor sharp.

Forward. We plant a stick
of nerve-paralyzing gas by the window
and set it off with a glass-shattering boom.
All inhabitants are paralyzed for fifteen minutes.
We race through the house calling Divina, Divina.
No Divina.
The mad dwarf doctor's eyes are bulging
and Madame Imperia's are glittering,
and Igor has murder in his—
for the gas does not put you out
and your brain goes right on figuring
and they were all thinking what to do about us
when the gas wore off:
They had a few tricks up their sleeves all right.

Minutes were ticking by. Ah, cages.
But we don't dare let loose the sub-human monsters there,
all operated on unsuccessfully by the mad Cranshaw.
Now a door to the basement, but sealed.
Search for a button in the wall.
No, not a button, an electric eye.

Break the beam and the door slides open.
Steps going down, an underground lab
with who? Yes, Divina
strapped to a table
breasts bulging up from thongs cutting into her flesh,
thighs writhing to protect her tender loins.

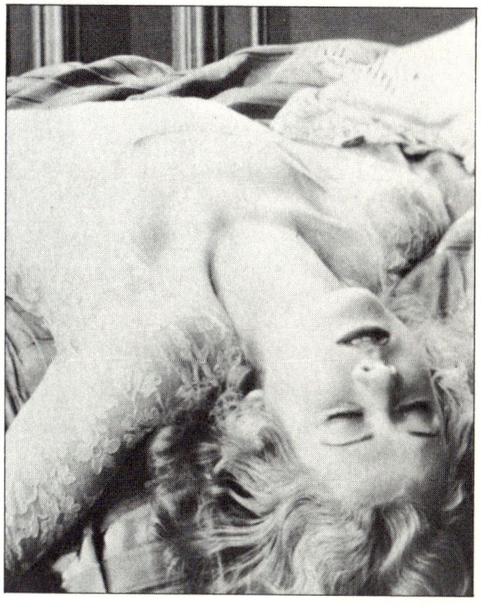

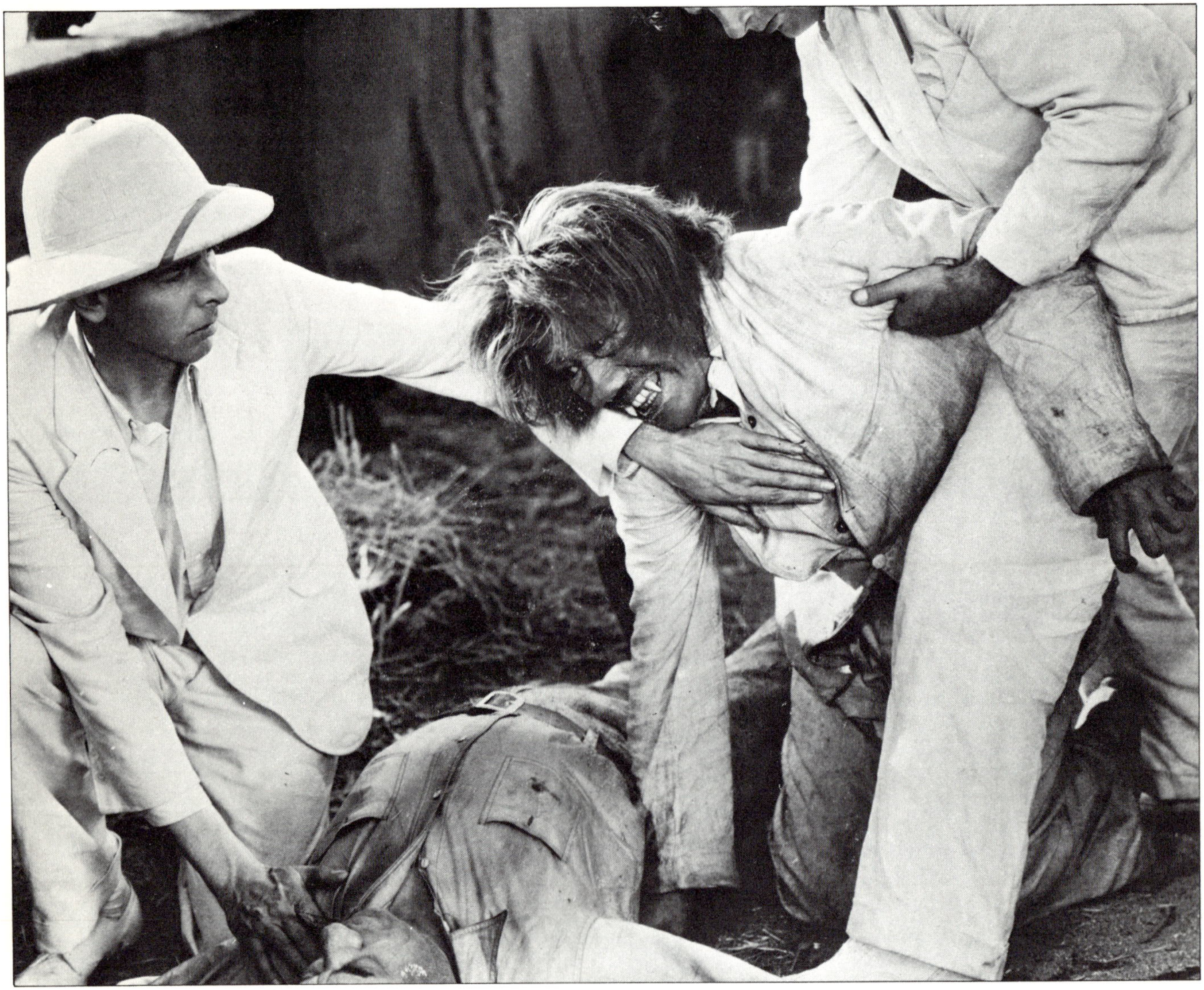

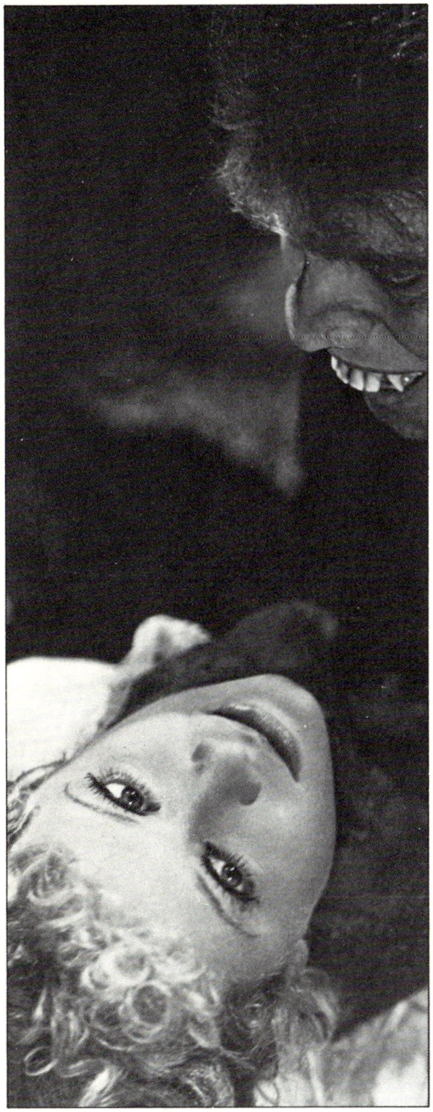

From the look of things
those dogmen had been having quite a go at her,
but apart from slaver on her face
and puddles of green dog come on her belly
it doesn't look like it has done her any harm
although she'll probably need a few weekends at Esalen
to straighten out her head.

Divina darling, I've come to free you.
But Divina's eyes are like stoned.
Has she been given a dog's brain already?

Oy, the fifteen minutes are up
and the whole pack of loonies burst in, grab us,
tie us up, and proceed with the operation.
There must be something to do, but it seems hopeless.

While the faithful Igor prepared the surgical instruments
and swung the great radiotrope into place
that directed the plastrons to the surgery,
the dwarf doctor took a great book off a bible-stand
and held it before us, turning the pages
while his eyes grew misty with memory:
"Here is my Book of the Dead," he said,
"the record of my experiments, my life work.
In the early stages I had such childish ideas,
that the serum could be made from blood and hair,
from flesh even." He riffled through
page after page of virgin sacrificed.
"But now I know it is a vibration one must catch.
I have the secret at last and tonight
I will finish my work: We will have the serum."
Madame Imperia could not resist giving a triumphant shriek.
"You mean," I said, "there will be no sacrifice of life?"
"No, she shall be alive and well . . . . . well, almost . . . ."
Here the mad dwarf faltered.

We strained at the bonds desperately. "What do you mean?"
"She will lack her. . . ah . . . her organ of generation."
"You mean you are taking out her cunt, you creep?" We blurted.
"A trifle. She'll be otherwise perfect.
My wife will be beautiful again after a few well-placed injections,
and I'll be free to go back to my original interest,
the study of the generative cycle of the four-toed wallaby."

The monster! Now I was really mad.
With my tongue I pried off the false cap of my right molar
putting into action a radio transmitter.
By clicking the teeth in morse code
messages could be sent.
"Isle of Dead mission calling Headquarters," I clicked.
I must have looked like I had a severe case of the chatters.
"Send choppers in at once."

Meanwhile the doctor continued with his work
zeroing the radiotrope right in to target.
There was no time to wait for helicopters, troops, medicaid—
I had to act.

There was an emergency capsule in one of my left molars—
I broke it out and swallowed.
It contained a special drug
to give five minutes of superhuman strength
but it had to be used with caution
because immediately after that you passed out.
I had to take care of this situation in five minutes—or else.
The drug coursed through my veins, my chest swelled,
I felt like superman to the rescue.
I snapped my bonds easily,
took Igor by the throat with one hand,
and Dr. Cranshaw with the other,
and tied them like a big sandwich
with Madame Imperia in-between clawing at them both.
And the pack of dogmen ran howling into the woods.

Of course I pulled the plug on the equipment at once.
And there was my Divina lying on the operating table,
her breasts bulging up at me, her eyes and wet lips

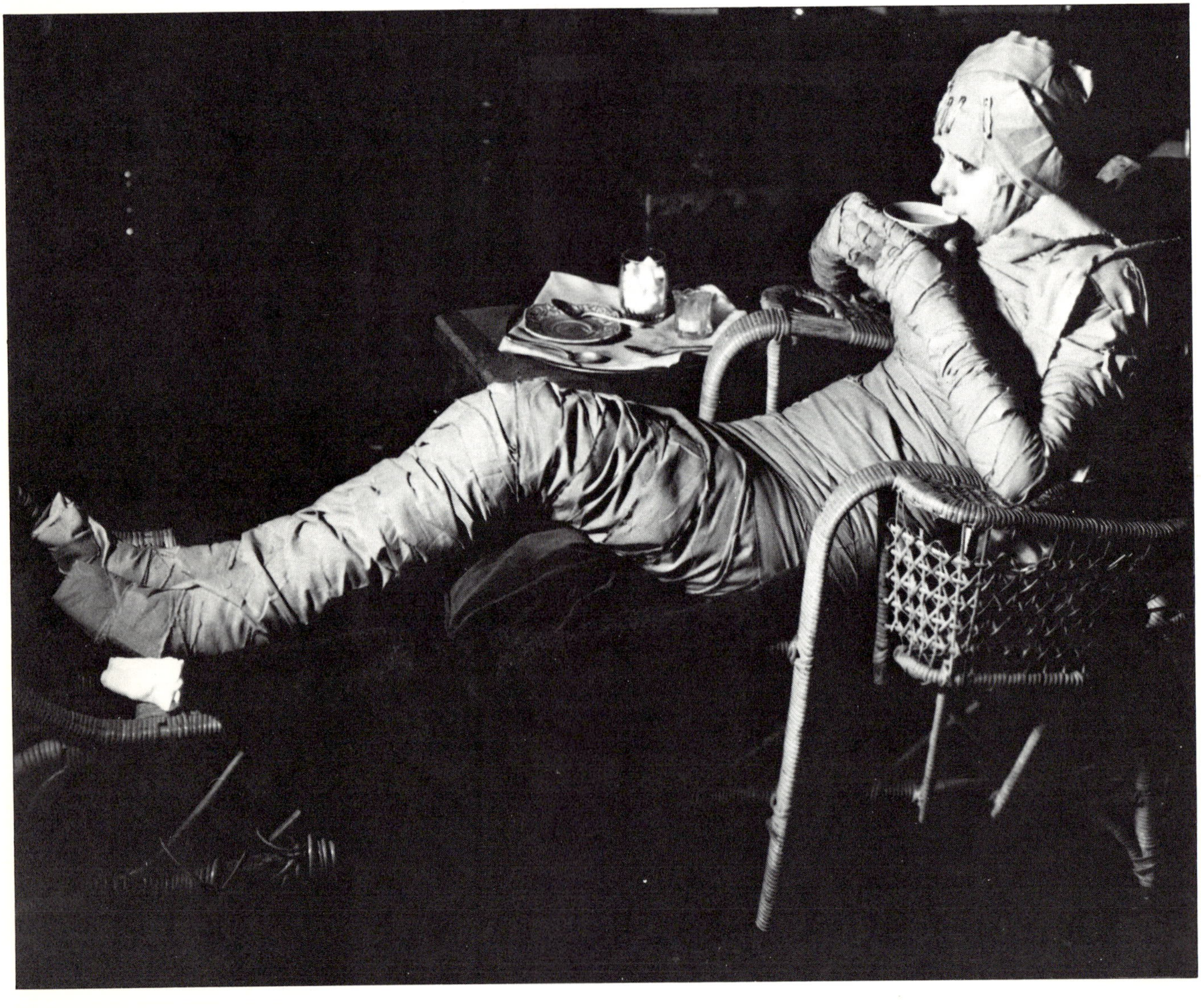

imploring me to come to her,
and with the superman drug in my veins
I had supersex to give her:
I felt it throbbing up in my loins.
That would bring her to her senses again if anything would.
When she saw the size of it she screemed,
then her brain clicked off, her eyes glazed,
and she started panting.
Give it to me, she moaned,
and ground her hips up as far as the thongs allowed her.
It's all for you baby, I said, and reached out
but she seemed to be getting further away from me.
I took bigger steps, but got slower and slower,
the earth whirled
and I slipped off into darkness.

When I awoke I was back at the stationhouse
on a couch in the locker room
and the Chief was leaning over me giving me a handjob saying,
Boy, you really need it bad.
I groaned and pushed him away.
Did you get Cranshaw and the others?

They're all behind bars
and we've got the dogcatcher rounding up the dogmen.
We hope to place them in good homes.
Divina has already made an application for a couple of them.

Where's Divina, Boss? Were we too late?

She'll be better than ever, Sonny,
once her cunt cools off.
The doc is putting icecubes up it.

And Madame Imperia?

She completely flipped out I'm afraid,
but you know, it's a mystery to me
because in the struggle to get ahold of her
her mask ripped off
and there was nothing wrong with her.
In fact, she was a darn goodlooking dame.

Then the doctor must have discovered the serum
but they were too crazy already
to know they had succeeded.
That book of his must be worth a fortune.

You mean the book he was raving about,
his Book of the Dead?

Yes, get it and put it under lock and key.
We're going to be on easy street.

Oh shit, Sonny, I guess I didn't tell you. .
There was a little fire—or rather a big one—
and the whole joint burned down—
you know those old houses.

Then our only hope is the doctor.
He'll know the secret.

The doctor? He's completely nuts.

Then I'd advise giving him a little laboratory to play around in
in the nuthouse, and a free hand
to experiment on the inmates
and a big book to write in.
I'll bet Revlon will finance the whole thing.

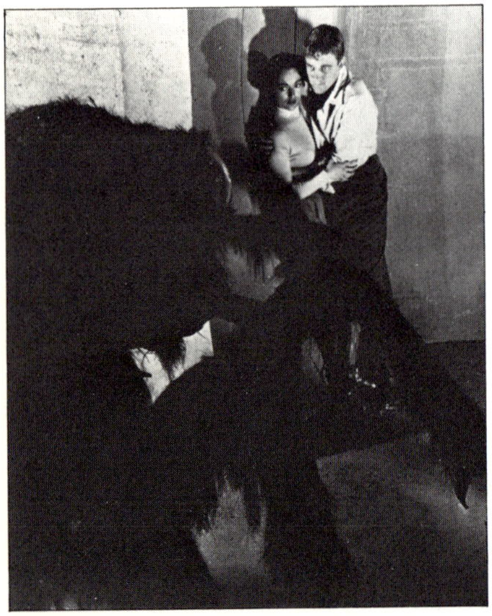

Just as the Chief turned back to his dirty picture book
with his hand stealing fondly into his open fly
the phone rang and he picked it up:
"What the hell you say? A thing? What kind of thing?
You say this thing came out of a lab at Caltech
when the chemicals were all spilled during the earthquake
and has been what? Eating co-eds
and getting bigger and bigger?
I thought it was a boys' school?
Oh, Women's Lib had a demonstration there and things changed . . . .
I'll send my man right over to investigate.
Yeah, he's the one who cracked the Cranshaw case.

So there went my vacation. I was on a new case,
one that would prove to be the toughest in my career,
fighting an extra-terrestrial blob
that made people into zombies . . . . .
but that's another story.

The Return of Frankenstein

He didn't die in the whirlpool by the mill
where he had fallen in after a wild chase
by all the people of the town.

Somehow he clung to an overhanging rock
until the villagers went away.

And when he came out, he was changed forever,
that soft heart of his had hardened
and he really was a monster now.

He was out to pay them back,
to throw the lie of brotherly love
in their white Christian teeth.

Wasn't his flesh human flesh
even made from the bodies of criminals,
the worst criminals the Baron could find?

But love is not necessarily implicit in human flesh:
Their hatred was now his hatred,

so he set out on his new career,
his previous one being the victim,
the good man who suffers.

Now no longer the hunted but the hunter
he was in charge of his destiny
and knew how to be cold and clever,

preserving barely a spark of memory
for the old blind musician
who once took him in and offered brotherhood.

His idea — if his career now had an idea —
was to kill them all,
keep them in terror anyway,
let them feel hunted.
Then perhaps they would look at others
with a little pity and love.

Only a suffering people have any virtue.

Stars in My Eyes

A limousine pulled up to Paradise Pictures
and a heavily veiled woman stepped out.
The studio guard hurried to open the great doors
and she swept in with a whispering of furs
straight through the ranks of secretaries
to the center of the hive
where T.L., top man at Paradise,
sat at his fabulous round desk with the sword hanging over it
which he claimed symbolized his expendability
but was said to be used on all rivals for his job.

Connie Comeback! he exclaimed, rising,
and came forward to take her warmly by both hands
and bring her into the heartland.
Why haven't we seen you in all these years?
Connie settled herself in a spiderweb chair,
pushed back her veils
to reveal the still-famous face lacquer perfect,
and lit a gold-tipped Fatima.
You haven't changed a bit, Connie, said T.L.
with genuine awe like before the Lincoln memorial.

STATE YOUR
BUSINESS
AND MAKE IT
SNAPPY
My Little Grey Home
in the East.
NO DOGS OR
PEDDLERS
ALLOWED

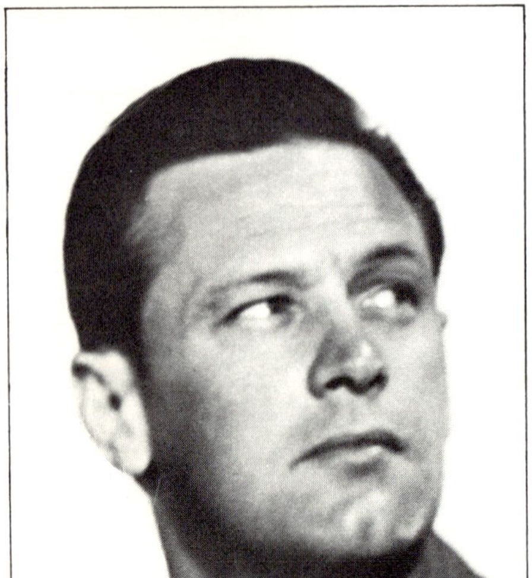

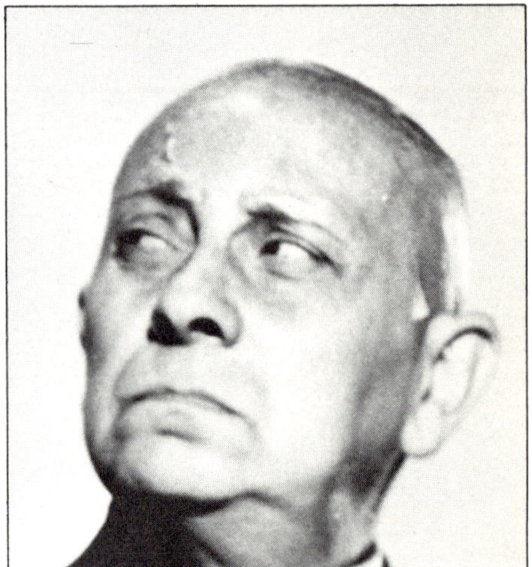

Sorry T.L., Vosberg was saying
in his heavy accent from the car phone,
she insisted on me driving her out to the studio
— I couldn't keep her home —
so string her along, will you?
Tell her you'll put her in a picture again, anything,
just keep her happy.
Tomorrow I'll tell her it was all a dream.
I've got her medicine ready:
As he spoke, he took a full cocktail shaker of martinis
out of the liquor cabinet built into the glove compartment
and dropped a knockout pill into it.

As T.L. hung up and thoughtfully turned back to his famous visitor
Connie was saying: I've found the perfect vehicle for my comeback,
and she produced a bulky manuscript from beneath her furs.
It's the story of a hillbilly girl
who is found by a psychiatrist on vacation in the woods.
He analyzes her for fun
and she becomes the leading international hostess
on the Washington political scene,
all the while secretly supporting
a bunch of half-wit relations in the cellar and attic!
You get the point? They can't change your soul.

Countess, you always come up with sure-fire ideas.
We really miss you here at the studio.
The new ones, they don't have glamour anymore.
(T.L. grew expansive with his wisdom.)
Hollywood is not a place, or even an industry.
It's the heart of America
and you are still enthroned there as queen.

You mean you want me back, T.L.?

Back, hell. Countess, you've never been away.
The boys on the lot still talk about you,
and if the technicians respect a star, she's a real star.

Haven't I, T.L.? She blew out a passionate cloud of smoke.
Then give me a picture. I'm ready to work again.
I was always good box office, wasn't I?

Number one B.O., Connie,
you packed them in and made millions for us
but. . . . The telephone interrupted him.

It was the great Vosberg, the director,
who was dedicating his life to Connie because he still loved her
although she had divorced him and gone on to six more husbands.
His tireless care alone kept her alive
for her compulsive rituals of beautification.
If Vosberg had once dreamed they would come out of retirement
that hope was long since dead: She was a lost cause.
But he knew that if she ever realized she was a has-been
her glass brain would shatter forever.

At the peak of her career, Connie, called Countess by friends,
went into complete retirement.
They had been filming Daylight Hours
in which she played the daytime mistress of a man
who had to stay home nights with his invalid wife.
The ingenue, Monica Mooner, playing the nothing role
of the man's secretary, stole every scene
with the wiggle of her young young body,
so Connie, impulsively, attacked her with a blow torch.

It was doing Monica a favor really
because her face wasn't star material
and this way plastic surgery could create for her
the perfect face she needed for her career.

Connie disappeared under heavy sedation
and Monica rose to fame and fortune in Daylight Hours,
though now she too was box office poison
and had joined the mah jong set in a bungalow colony
waiting for the call from the studio that never came.

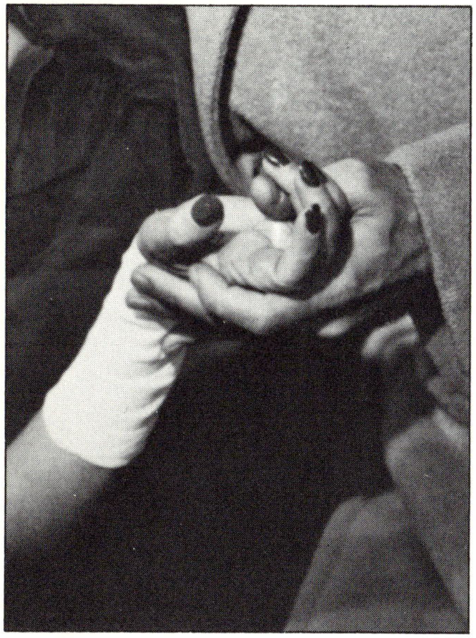

And T.L. picked up a microphone,
switching off the loudspeaker system under his desk,
and with a tremor in his voice and real tears in his eyes
announced that Connie Comeback would make her comeback
in The Upstairs and Downstairs of the Heart.
If the best-seller shook the nation
the movie would go off like an atomic bomb!

He pressed a button and flashbulbs popped around them
while from a loudspeaker came applause and cheers.
Tears of gratitude rolled darkly down Connie's cheeks.
They still wanted her . . . they wanted her back . . .
She straightened up proudly: Hell, she's never been away!

Then like a liner guided from the dock by tugboats
and salutes from shore guns and crowds and flags
Connie Comeback leaned back in her long limousine
waving a gloved hand at her millions of fans
and left the studio
sipping her cocktail of forgetfulness.

Credits: The photographs used to illustrate *Stars in My Eyes* come from the following films: *A Song to Remember; A Woman's Face; The Black Cat; Bride of Frankenstein; The Bride Wore Red; The Curse of Frankenstein; Dawn Patrol; Dr. Jekyll and Mr. Hyde; Female on the Beach; Frankenstein; Island of Lost Souls; The Jolson Story; King Kong; Old Clothes; Paris; The Return of Frankenstein; Rhapsody in Blue; She; Strange Cargo; Sunset Boulevard; Trader Horn;* and *The Women.* Studio portraits and candid photographs are of Mae West, Sonja Henie, Joan Crawford, Clara Bow, Mary Pickford, Louise Brooks, Lillian Gish, Leatrice Joy, and Gloria Swanson.